Mama of the Nation

The Story of Cecilia Tamanda Kadzamira and the Values that Guide Her Life

Written by
Stephanie Kaye Wezeman
Phyllis Vos Wezeman

With
Chrissy Linda Kadzamira

Illustrated by
David Blodgett

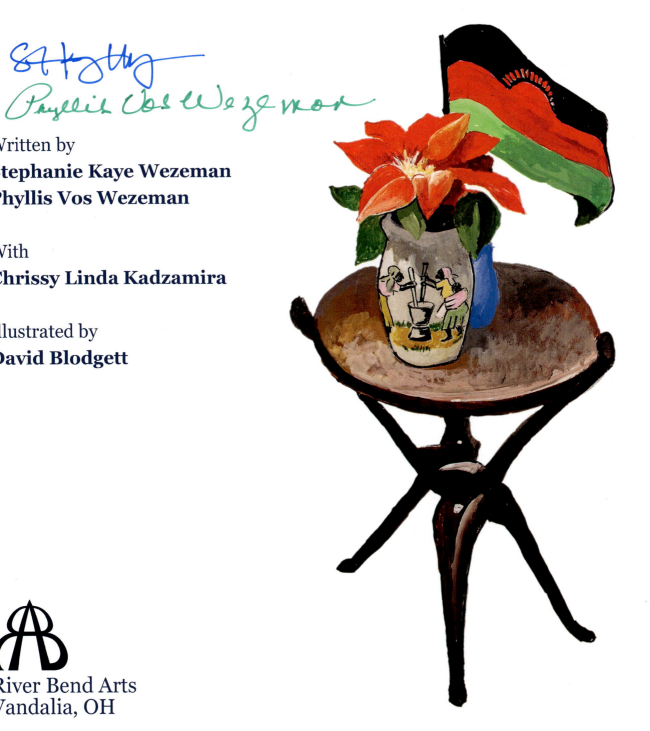

River Bend Arts
Vandalia, OH

ZIKOMO KWAMBIRI

For friendship and support
Chrissy Linda Kadzamira

For conviction and courage
John Wycliffe Lameck Kadzamira (In Loving Memory)
Ethel Malemia Kadzamira

For encouragement and hospitality
Jean H. Kadzamira Kalinga
Beatrice Kadzamira
Catherine Kadzamira Mgangira
Doris Kadzamira Chikoti
Esme Kadzamira
Rosemary Kadzamira (In Loving Memory)
Tamanda Kadzamira Chakhumbira
Clement Chimwemwe Kadzamira

For research assistance
Lucy Kadzamira (In Loving Memory)
Dowell Nyondo at Kamuzu Academy

While conducting research for this book, we found many sources to be contradictory or unreliable. When unsure, we opted to use information as provided by Mama Cecilia's family and friends.

Mama of the Nation: The Story of Cecilia Tamanda Kadzamira
by Stephanie Kaye Wezeman and Phyllis Vos Wezeman
with Chrissy Linda Kadzamira
illustrations by David Blodgett and Stephanie Kaye Wezeman
Text copyright © 2021 by Stephanie Kaye Wezeman and Phyllis Vos Wezeman
Art copyright © 2021 by River Bend Arts

ISBN-13: 978-1-953901-00-2
Library of Congress Control Number: 2020925626

All rights reserved. No part of this publication may be reproduced or transmitted in any form or by any means, electronic or mechanical, including photocopying, recording, or any information storage or retrieval system, without prior permission in writing from the publisher. Permission is hereby given to use short excerpts with proper citation in reviews.

Layout and Design by River Bend Arts
Printed in the United States of America by Total Printing Systems, 2021

River Bend Arts
P.O. Box 742
Vandalia, OH 45377
riverbendarts.net

To Destiny Upile Matupa —

Your great-great aunt Cecilia has been an inspiration, role-model, and friend to millions. We are honored to tell her story and to watch her legacy continue in you.

Daughter
mwana wamkazi

Gratitude filled Lameck and Milika Tembo Kadzamira's hearts when their daughter Cecilia was born on March 10, 1937 at Nkhoma Mission Hospital in Nyasaland, Africa. Cecilia's father worked in the pharmacy and her mother was the daughter of a church minister.

Cecilia's parents chose the Chewa middle name *Tamanda*, meaning *Praise the Lord*. God, family, and education were priorities for the Kadzamiras and they raised their children with strong values.

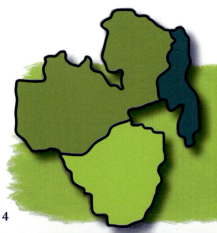

Before independence, Malawi was part of the British Federation of Rhodesia and Nyasaland.

- July 6, 1964 - Nyasaland became Malawi
- October 24, 1964 - Northern Rhodesia became Zambia
- April 18, 1980 - Southern Rhodesia became Zimbabwe

Values

Every family has values that guide their lives.

Name three values that are important to your family.

Sister

chemwali

When Cecilia was still a toddler, the family moved to Southern Rhodesia. There were long periods of separation while the older children stayed in Nyasaland with their grandparents *Abusa* and *Amayi* Tembo for school, but the brothers and sisters developed strong bonds throughout their lives.

Cecilia's household of eleven had close ties with family and friends in two countries. When they gathered to celebrate weddings, holidays, and prayers, they prepared traditional dishes like *nsima*, a food made from corn that is ground into a fine flour.

The Kadzamira Family
Lameck Misheck Kadzamira, Milika Tembo Kadzamira, Eunice, John, George, Lucy, Cecilia, Mary, David, Esnath, William

Connection

Families stay connected in many ways.
Share some traditions that keep your family close.

Student

wophunzira

Classes at Mbisi Primary, Cecilia's school in Salisbury, were taught in English. She studied hard and earned top marks. It wasn't all work, though. Cecilia enjoyed playing netball, a game similar to basketball.

All the Kadzamira children attended British schools, pursued higher education, and worked in careers of great responsibility.

School
Students in Malawi do not call their school years Grades 1-12. They attend Primary School for Standards 1-8 and Secondary School for Forms 1-4.

Excellence

Being successful requires hard work and extra effort.
Discuss how you give your personal best.

Cadet

wophunzira-unamwino

Cecilia followed in her father's footsteps by choosing a career in the medical field. Mr. Kadzamira enrolled his daughter in a two-year training program in Midwifery at Salisbury General Hospital.

Later, Cecilia moved back to Nyasaland and completed her nursing training at Zomba General Hospital.

Midwife
Midwives take care of expectant mothers and help keep moms and babies safe during childbirth.

Purpose

Cecilia decided helping others was her purpose in life.
Dream about goals you have for your future.

Nurse

namwino

Cecilia stayed in Nyasaland to begin her nursing career. Her first job was with Dr. Hastings Kamuzu Banda at Limbe Surgery Centre.

Dr. Banda had recently returned to his homeland with three goals: practice medicine, release his country from the federation with Northern and Southern Rhodesia, and prepare Nyasaland for independence from Great Britain.

A bright, hard-working, dedicated woman, Cecilia became indispensable to Dr. Banda and took on many responsibilities.

Dr. Hastings Kamuzu Banda
Dr. Banda was born 15 February 1898 in Nyasaland and died 25 November 1997 in South Africa. He was Prime Minister of Malawi from 1964-1966 and President of the Republic from 1966-1994.

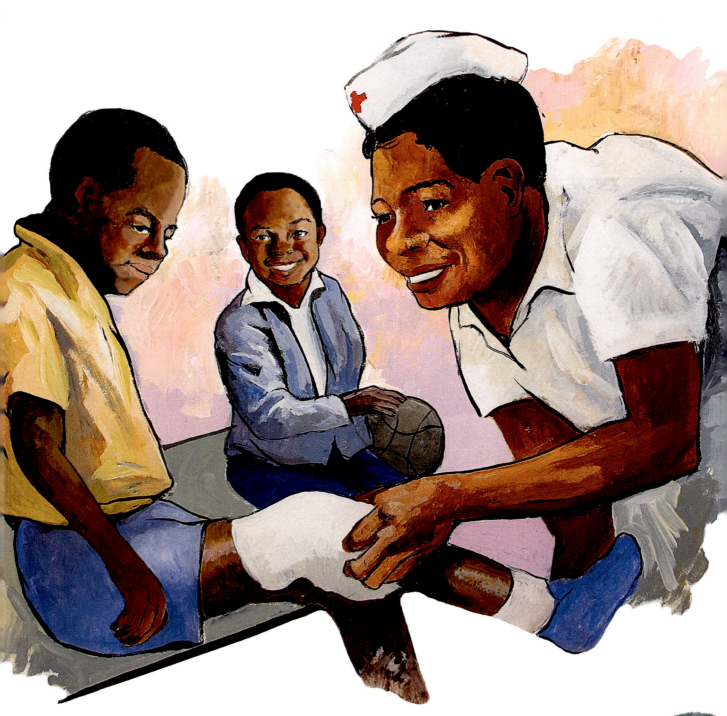

Dedication

It takes hard work to be successful.

Talk about a time you kept trying until you succeeded.

Official Government Hostess

 wolemekezeka aboma

Cecilia's job changed when Dr. Banda became Prime Minister of Malawi. She moved to Zomba to work as his private secretary, running the day-to-day affairs of the government.

A few years later, Dr. Banda became President of the newly independent Republic of Malawi. Since he was not married, the country was without a First Lady. Cecilia Tamanda Kadzamira was named the Official Government Hostess. In her new role, she managed the State House and became responsible for Malawi's social and diplomatic activities.

Malawi's flag has three horizontal stripes:
- black for the indigenous people of Africa.
- red for the blood shed for independence.
- green for the vegetation of the country.

The rising sun represents freedom and hope.

Responsibility

New opportunities bring unique responsibilities.
Tell how you serve as a helper for others.

Mama of the Nation

mayi wa fuko

President Banda soon gave Cecilia a less formal and more traditional title: Mama of the Nation. In East African culture, women are called "Auntie" or "Mama" as a sign of respect. To raise Cecilia from Hostess to Mama signified her level of responsibility in the government. It also indicated the trust placed in her by President Banda and the people of Malawi.

Languages
While English and Chichewa are the official languages of Malawi, a total of nine are nationally recognized. Thank you—*zikomo* in Chichewa—is the most important word to know in any language. *Mphatso* means gift.

Appreciation

President Banda honored Cecilia every time he used the phrase "Mama and I" at events.

Think of ways to honor people you appreciate.

Ambassador

kazembe

Cecilia's bright smile offered a warm welcome for visitors amid the hustle and bustle of life at the State House. She managed residences, conducted meetings, coordinated banquets, and oversaw diplomatic travel with efficiency and grace.

Mama developed close ties with the First Ladies of Zambia and Zimbabwe, ensuring that all three former members of the Federation of Rhodesia and Nyasaland continued to work together for the betterment of the region. Malawi also maintained good relations with the United Kingdom and other countries of the world.

The Warm Heart of Africa
Malawi is known as "The Warm Heart of Africa" because visitors are greeted with warmth, generosity, and kindness.

Hospitality
Offering hospitality to visitors is valued by all cultures.
Explain the ways that you make others feel welcome.

Leader

m'tsogoleri

Cecilia's hospitality was not limited to official visitors. President Banda counted on her to spend time with the people of Malawi, inspiring them to support his mission. Mama traveled throughout the country explaining his four values known as cornerstones or pillars: Discipline, Loyalty, Obedience, and Unity.

The Four Pillars
President Banda presented his vision for Malawi through four cornerstones called pillars. He asked the citizens to show discipline in their behavior, loyalty to the nation, obedience to the law, and unity as a people.

Vision

Mama worked hard to share a vision for Malawi with the people. Suggest ways you help people understand your ideas.

Advocate

nkhoswe

In addition to presenting four pillars, President Banda identified four enemies, or evils, and their solutions. Mama Cecilia challenged the people of Malawi to become responsible for fighting disease, ending hunger, reducing ignorance, and overcoming poverty.

Cecilia encouraged her people to embrace their independence from colonial rule. Mama connected Malawi's citizens with government offices and charitable organizations that built schools, developed small businesses, opened health centers, and taught farming practices.

Evils
- disease
- hunger
- ignorance
- poverty

Solutions
- health care
- farming
- education
- business

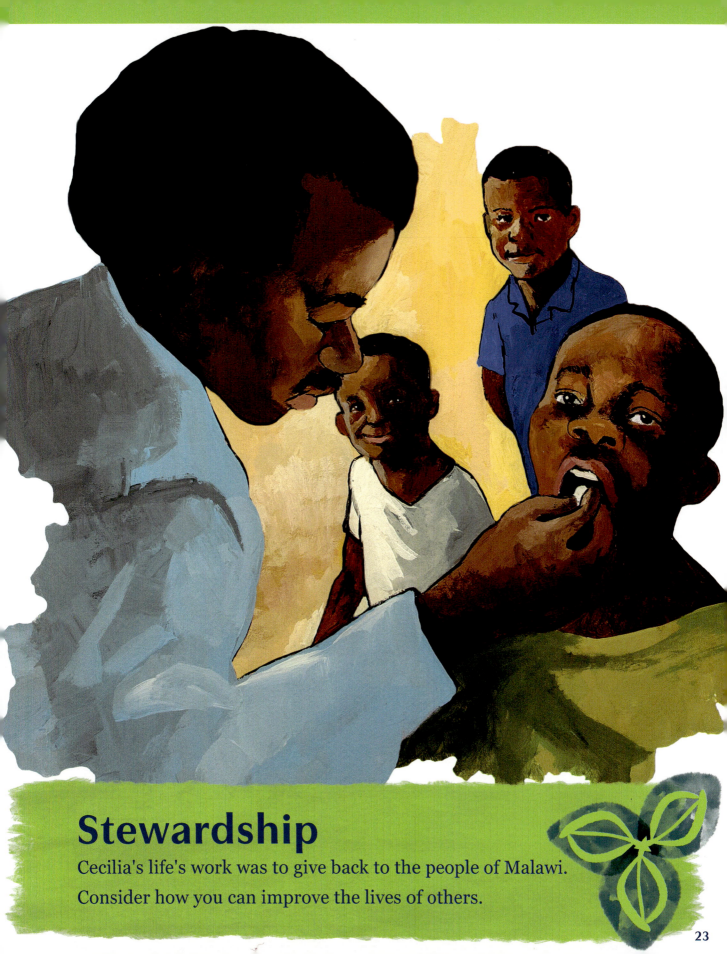

Stewardship

Cecilia's life's work was to give back to the people of Malawi. Consider how you can improve the lives of others.

Advisor
mlangizi

Child marriage is a world-wide concern. According to UNICEF, this human rights violation causes problems such as domestic abuse, limited education, and high-risk pregnancies.

21% of girls on the globe are married before age 18.

46% of Malawian girls are child brides.

Cecilia understood that when women's lives are better, everyone's lives improve. In the 1980s, she took on the position of National Advisor of *Chitukuko Cha Amayi Malawi* - CCAM, a government department dedicated to elevating the role of women in society.

CCAM encouraged women to finish school, even if they were already wives and mothers. Doing so allowed them and their families to enjoy healthier, more prosperous lives. CCAM also stressed leading a moral life and obeying the laws of the land.

Improvement

Advisors help people become the best they can be.
Recall people who have helped you make good choices.

Activist
~ womenyera ~

Cecilia's commitment to the people of Malawi did not end when Dr. Banda left the office of President. While she no longer held the title of Official Government Hostess, she remained Mama of the Nation.

Mama Cecilia serves on the Board of Trustees of Kamuzu Academy, promotes reforestation, advocates sustainable farming, supports child welfare, champions health care, participates in the Women's Guild of her church, and works with countless organizations that share her passion for the Malawian people.

Agriculture
Farming is the foundation of Malawi's economy. Many people grow ground nuts, maize, and potatoes to feed their families and sell in the village. Crops such as tea, sugar, and tobacco are shipped around the world.

Generosity

Cecilia has always been generous with her time and talent.

List special skills you use to work with others.

Role Model

chifanizo

Cecilia Kadzamira is admired around the globe for her dedication to the people of Malawi and the world. Malawi honored Mama with a Women of Distinction Lifetime Achiever Award and the Order of the Lion of Malawi.

Mama Cecilia drew inspiration from other women as she embraced her place as a role model. Ruth and Esther from the Bible, Queen Elizabeth II of Great Britain, Queen Sirikit of Thailand, and her own mother offered examples for how to accept her calling, serve with dignity, and live a life of integrity.

values, vision, connection, excellence, purpose, improvement, dedication, responsibility, hospitality, generosity, integrity, appreciation, stewardship

What values have you learned from Mama Cecilia?
How will you share them with others?

Integrity

Mama Cecilia models values learned from her role models.
Reflect on lessons learned from examples in your life.

In all of the roles Cecilia Tamanda Kadzamira has filled throughout her life, her values have shone through. The most important one, the value that guides all others, has come from her heart. Her love for God, family, the people of Malawi, and the world inspires everything she does.

Mama's legacy is **LOVE** and that's a legacy worth living.

Our Connection to Malawi

Phyllis Vos Wezeman

July 21, 2006, the last day of my second trip to Malawi was the first day of a lifelong friendship with Cecilia Tamanda Kadzamira, the aunt of Chrissy Kadzamira, a member of my church in South Bend, Indiana. Now, twenty-three trips later (2020), spending time with Mama Cecilia is a highlight of each visit. As President of the not-for-profit Malawi Matters, I've benefited from Mama's insights that enhance our mission. As an author/educator, I dreamed of sharing a story of the values that shape Mama's life. On March 14, 2012 I told her my idea for a children's book and she replied, "You can do it." Thus, *Mama of the Nation* grew from vision to reality.

Stephanie Kaye Wezeman

The purpose of my first trip to Malawi was to train community leaders in creative methods of HIV/AIDS education. Mama's niece Chrissy, friend and fellow Malawi Matters board member, told me to expect warmth and generosity. Malawi lived up to its reputation as "The Warm Heart of Africa"—from the small village of Chibanzi to Mama Cecilia's home in Lilongwe. I'm honored to tell Mama's story and grateful that my students and those in Malawi will learn from her example.

Our Format for the Book

Two-page spreads convey the story of Cecilia Tamanda Kadzamira (/**käd**-zə-mir-ə/), from birth through current, ongoing activities. A title word describes Mama at each stage of life followed by a Chichewa translation of the word to ground the story in Malawi and introduce readers outside of East Central Africa to a beautiful language rarely spoken beyond that region. A brief story about Mama focuses on the role mentioned in the title. The topic continues with a word to describe a value illustrated in each part of Mama's life and a challenge for the reader to follow her example. A sidebar provides additional information related to the story.

Framing the story are images of our friend Destiny, Chrissy's granddaughter, Mama Cecilia's great-great niece. While the book is dedicated to Destiny, our goal is that readers will put themselves in the picture and illustrate Mama's values in their own lives.